REBEL BELIEVERS

CONFRONTING THE WORLD WITH CHRISTIAN OPTIMISM

REBEL BELIEVERS

CONFRONTING THE WORLD WITH CHRISTIAN OPTIMISM

Paul Graas

Scepter

Published by Scepter Publishers, Inc.
info@scepterpublishers.org
www.scepterpublishers.org
800-322-8773
New York

Cover design by Rose Design
Page design and composition by Rose Design

Paperback ISBN: 978-1-59417-548-0
Ebook ISBN: 978-1-59417-549-7
Library of Congress Control Number: 2025933383

Printed in the United States of America

Contents

Introduction

> Character—the willingness to accept responsibility for one's own life—is the source from which self-respect springs.
>
> —Joan Didion[1]

Aldous Huxley wrote his famous book *Brave New World* in 1932. That book is about a society dominated by technology, rationalism, and hedonism. There is no war or poverty and everyone seems to live a healthy and happy life. Traditional values such as fidelity, love, family life, art, and religion no longer exist, nor does the free choice of an individual have any place in this society. All the world lives this way. There are only a few areas left—so-called savage reservations—where people still live

1. Joan Didion, "On Self Respect," in *Slouching Towards Bethlehem* (Farrar, Straus and Giroux, 1968), p. 145.

according to traditional values in a primitive society: Families exist, they have religions, they get sick, and they suffer pain.

Due to circumstances, a young man from one such savage reservation ends up in the "beautiful new world." Soon he becomes a kind of attraction for everyone, like an exotic animal in a zoo. He gradually begins to loathe and hate this world. He simply cannot believe that such a society exists.

I do identify a bit with this young man. At least, I understand his feelings. After all, I am a practicing Catholic living in a Western country in the twenty-first century. And that sometimes makes me feel like an oddball: someone still living with a backward worldview, in which a hierarchical institution founded by Jesus Christ tells him how to live. The morality proclaimed to him is also, in some cases, diametrically opposed to much that is commonly accepted in contemporary Western culture.

It is not comfortable to live with that conviction. You can deal with it in different ways: You can shut yourself up in your parish, build your social life there and ignore the world around it. You can adopt a cynical attitude and be content with the fact that the decadent Western world is going down. Or you can come to the conclusion that it makes no sense and that it is better to get off the church boat and seek peace and safety on the mainland of prevailing worldly ideas.

There is also an alternative: As a Christian you confront this world with optimism as a witness to the eternal message of Christ. You show with your life that the Church exists to unite heaven and earth, with the goal of achieving man's ultimate happiness. You resolve, with Christ in your heart, to love this world, not just tolerate it.

This book is written to help you travel on this path, because it demands a lot to follow it: nothing less than all of your life! It is worth the effort, and desperately needed, for the Church and for all the world. Today's evangelization will happen much less inside the church and much more in the streets, among all kinds of people. The most beautiful and effective evangelization is that of a person with the divinity and humanity of Christ.

1
CHAPTER

Authentic Ideals

All people on earth crave happiness. All people on earth yearn for the meaning of life. All people on earth hope that their lives are worth more than a tombstone after they die. The question is: How do you achieve that happiness? What path should you take to reach your life ideals?

The more authentic, deep, and beautiful an ideal is, the happier you can become. And there is nothing more authentic, deep, and beautiful than true love. The apostle Paul writes a beautiful hymn about love in his first letter to the Corinthians. It is worth considering quietly:

> If I speak in the tongues of men and of angels, but have not love, I am a noisy gong or a clanging

> cymbal . . . Love is patient and kind; love is not jealous or boastful; it is not arrogant or rude. Love does not insist on its own way; it is not irritable or resentful; it does not rejoice at wrong, but rejoices in the right. Love bears all things, believes all things, hopes all things, endures all things. (1 Cor 13:1, 4–7)

What St. Paul is trying to make clear to us is that life is worth nothing if it is not based on love. You can go on the most impressive world trips, be very popular in your social circle, pursue the best career, find the nicest life partner. . . . If all this does not make you want to love more, then you are wasting your time. And by love, I don't mean a *like* you give to someone's picture on social media, nor some kind of chill feeling you can get from doing a fun project. Love is effort, sacrifice, generosity. It is openness to the truth.

Why do I put so much emphasis on this? Because there is a misconception in today's society (even among Christians!) that the road to happiness is easy and comfortable, and that you should think a lot about yourself above all else. In other words, that an easy life is enough to become happy. Nothing could be further from the truth! The way to happiness is through the cross, with self-forgetfulness and self-surrender. I will elaborate on this conviction in the following chapters. But for now, I want to share with you the following words about love and holiness:

> The saints were saints because they were cheerful when it was difficult to be cheerful, patient when it was difficult to be patient, silent when they wanted to speak, and agreeable when they felt an urge to scream. They pushed forward when they wanted to stand still. Sainthood is simply another word for self-forgetfulness and generosity.[1]

I want to encourage you to think about the ideals that motivate your life. Where do you want to go? Do you settle for an easy, mediocre life or do you want to strive for grand ideals? Do you want to be a person who is comfortable floating with the crowd, or are you willing to swim against it? Don't worry about

---

1. Lawrence G. Lovasik, *The Hidden Power of Kindness* (Sophia Institute Press, 1999), pp. 30–31.

the question of how, yet. We will dwell on that in the following chapters. For now it is especially important to discover whether you have that desire to strive for greatness, whether you want to love with all your soul and all your body.

Perhaps the following text from the Spanish philosopher José Ortega y Gasset will help focus your thinking:

> The most radical division that is possible to make of humanity is that which splits it into two classes of creatures: those who make great demands on themselves, piling up difficulties and duties; and those who demand nothing special of themselves, but for whom to live is to be every moment what they already are, without imposing on themselves any effort towards perfection; mere buoys that float on the waves.[2]

A person with great ideals, who is not limited by laziness or others' opinions, but who is seeking true

---

2. José Ortega y Gasset, *The Revolt of the Masses* (W. W. Norton & Company, 1994), p. 15.

and genuine love, is a person capable of discovering Christ. An ancient Catholic hymn reads, *Ubi caritas et amor, Deus ibi est.* In English, it means: “Where charity and love are, God is there.”

Christians with authentic ideals stand on the same ground as everyone else. We long for the same happiness as everyone else and cherish noble ambitions: faithful friends, a fulfilling job, a happy marriage and family, hobbies, exploring the world, and so on. But a Christian tries to discover behind all this the face of a Person, and that is Jesus Christ. These “earthly” ambitions are not goals that stand alone, but gain their true meaning in the eternal love of God. The Holy Spirit makes use of all the beauty that our hearts desire to meet you and me personally. A small-minded and distrustful person leaves little room to find God. On the other hand, if a person seeks true love in all his ideals, his heart opens wide to Christ’s love.

The apostle Paul writes that before the world was made, God chose us to be happy in Christ (Eph 1:4). Every human being longs for this, though many do not know it. St. Augustine expressed this longing beautifully in his *Confessions*: "You have made us for yourself, and our heart is restless until it rests in you."[3] A person of character takes responsibility for the destiny of their life. They are determined to discover Christ in their life and to focus their existence entirely on him. They use all means to imbue their earthly existence with Christ's divine identity.

The most authentic ideal a human being can have on earth is the love of God, because we are created for that ideal.

3. Augustine, *Confessions*, trans. Henry Chadwick (Oxford, 2009), 1.1.

2

CHAPTER

Hard Work

I grew up and live in the Netherlands. In this small European country, the chances are high that you are well off in terms of economic and social prosperity. You can enjoy a good education; and with a little effort you can finish your degree and find a reasonable job. You enjoy good healthcare; and you live in a free and stable democracy.

It is good to be grateful for all that you have been given, but it's dangerous to stop at being satisfied with what you possess. Even more dangerous is the idea that a comfortable life and minimal effort are enough to achieve deep happiness. Deep happiness is not achieved by laziness, but by hard work. So said Charles Dickens in his book *David Copperfield*:

> I have never believed it possible that any natural or improved ability can claim immunity from the companionship of the steady, plain, hard-working qualities, and hope to gain its end. There is no such thing as such fulfilment on this earth. Some happy talent, and some fortunate opportunity, may form the two sides of the ladder on which some men mount, but the rungs of that ladder must be made of stuff to stand wear and tear. There is no subtitute for thorough-going, ardent, and sincere earnestness.[1]

To overcome obstacles and setbacks, you have to form virtues. But what virtues? And why are they so important? One of the best-known classical definitions is that virtue is a good operative habit, and these habits form the heart. They cause the heart to have a disposition that makes it desire the good, the beautiful, the true. A person who has exercised himself to get up every day on time, to be sincere and honest, to

1. Charles Dickens, *David Copperfield* (Oxford, 2008), pp. 590–591.

study at the appointed time, or to listen attentively to others, is a person who forges virtues such as punctuality, sincerity, order, and justice, so that they take root in his character and form the heart. And, of course, the reverse also applies. A person who never gets up on time, who is accustomed to lying when it is convenient, who postpones his duties, who does not make an effort to listen to others, is a person who gradually becomes lazy, dishonest, disorderly, and unjust.

Many philosophers and theologians over the centuries have pondered on the importance of virtues, such as the Greek philosophers Plato and Aristotle. They claimed that virtues are the way to a happy life, and that there are four core virtues that are assumed in every other virtue. These are justice, temperance, strength, and prudence. In other words, a person who is just, temperate, strong, and prudent is happy according to Plato and Aristotle.

The beauty of the Christian tradition is that it has built upon the wisdom these philosophers discovered with the light of reason. The virtue teachings of the ancient Greeks are the foundation on which we can build to become happy. But the Church says that the edifice of happiness is not yet complete with these virtues. The cardinal virtues that man can make his own through his own efforts form the foundation. There are also virtues that man cannot attain by his own strength, but can only receive from God. These divine virtues are faith, hope, and love.

Ground Dweller vs. Cloud Dweller

It is important to reflect on this for a moment when we consider the Christian faith and the desire for happiness. Because there are several pitfalls a Christian can fall into. One I call that of the "ground" dweller. You fall into this pit if you think you can achieve true happiness by your own strength. You keep your feet on the ground, thinking you can ascend to heaven by yourself. A second is that of the "cloud" dweller. You think that you yourself can do nothing, and you make no effort to make something of your life. You think it will all be given to you from above. Your thoughts are floating with the sky, but your feet are not on the ground.

We will talk more about the ground dweller later. For now the cloud dweller will be the focus. For this chapter is focused on the Christian who wants to work hard, and the cloud dweller is a person who talks a lot about the faith, hope, and love of God, but gives little effort to make something of his life. This is not a good Christian, for a good Christian is one who struggles to make the cardinal virtues his own.

The Lord tells us a beautiful parable in the Gospel of Matthew that is worth thinking about:

> Every one then who hears these words of mine and does them will be like a wise man who built his house upon the rock; and the rain fell, and the floods came, and the winds blew and beat upon that house, but it did not fall, because it had been founded on the rock. And every one who hears these words of mine and does not do them will be like a foolish man who built his house upon the sand; and the rain fell, and the floods came, and the winds blew and beat against that house, and it fell; and great was the fall of it. (Mt 7: 24–27)

We read here about two men. Both had a beautiful ideal, building a house, but the way they wanted to achieve their ideal was different. The first chose the hard way. He built his house on rock. The second chose the easy way and built his house on sand.

The question is: What exactly are that rock and sand in the Lord's parable? What is the house? And how can we apply this story to our own lives? The rock represents the virtues we can achieve through our own efforts. The house represents the divine virtues. A person who works hard to make human virtues their own and builds the house of divine ideals together with the Holy Spirit is a person who is able to make the Word of God their own and act accordingly in their daily life. This person will not give up at the first setback in life. They have developed character. They will persevere even when it takes effort.

The fool in this parable is the person who may have ideals, perhaps great divine ideals, but who is not willing to work hard. This person is the cloud dweller. The cloud dweller does profess that he believes in Christ and that God's mercy is infinite, but at the slightest setback he gets self-pity and gives up. For example, if he has had a bad day, he reacts grumpily to his surroundings. The cloud dweller is such a fool. He sings along fervently in church on Sundays, but outside church he is a lukewarm and mediocre person, and at the first setback his hope, faith, and love collapse.

If we look at the life of Christ, we see that for most of his life, he lived a very ordinary and hardworking existence; a discreet and simple life in Nazareth, together with Mary and Joseph. I cannot imagine him sitting on the couch all day, using a magic wand to do housework for Mary and make tables and chairs for Joseph. He worked hard! He patiently learned his earthly father's craft to eventually help him with the carpentry. He listened attentively to Mary's wise maternal advice to shape his character. Of the thirty-three years he spent on earth, he lived a hidden and hardworking life for thirty years to show you and me the right path. How else do you think the Lord was able to walk the way to the Cross? Do you think the angels protected him from all the difficulties in his last three years on earth? Do you think he did not feel the pain of the lashes and nails?

Christ built his divine house on the rock of his daily existence in Nazareth. He made it into something concrete and human. The philosopher Peter Kreeft writes:

> Our faith is true, and precious, and priceless, but it is not *heavy* enough. It is like a beautiful golden cloud. When life deposits a heavy burden on us, it falls through the cloud like a cannonball because it is heavier than any cloud, even a golden one. Our faith must become more than a cloud; it must become a *thing*, a thing more real and solid and substantial than any burden.[2]

The miracles of faith, hope, and love will be performed in your life if you are willing to work hard like Jesus, the son of Mary and Joseph.

The famous British writer C. S. Lewis once said in an interview that he did not seek refuge in religion

---

2. Peter Kreeft, *The Philosophy of Jesus* (St. Augustine's Press, 2007), p. 109.

for the good feeling. For that—he said—it is better to drink a bottle of port.[3] Christianity is not the place to be if you are looking for a religion that preaches a comfortable life, because Christianity says that you have to work hard day in and day out to become a man or woman of virtues, because only in this way will you be able to follow Christ, the carpenter's son, on his way to the Resurrection.

3. C. S. Lewis, *God in the Dock* (Eerdmans, 2014), pp. 47–48.

3
CHAPTER

Fall and Get Up

Many fairy tales, novels, and movies have a certain pattern to the story. At the beginning, you are introduced to the main character and their life. At some point, that character faces a major challenge. Everything seems to be going well, but at some point there is a crisis or a confrontation. The main character fails to overcome the difficulties. They seem to be about to give up, but eventually (often with the help of others) they decide to face the challenge again and this time they overcome it.

This pattern is very recognizable to everyone because it is something we all face, both in big and small things. Think of everyday things like getting up when the alarm clock rings, studying for an exam, or wanting to lose weight. And also special things like winning the heart of someone you love. You make the resolution, you go for it, but then difficulties and setbacks come. Sometimes you don't manage to overcome those difficulties. You fail in your resolutions. Then comes the essential question: How do you deal with it? Such situations are the best measure of a person's character.

In the book *Oathbringer* by fantasy writer Brandon Sanderson, one of the main characters tells the following:

> A journey will have pain and failure. It is not only the steps forward that we must accept. It is the stumbles. The trials. The knowledge that we will fail. That we will hurt those around us. But if we stop, if we accept the person we are when we fall, the journey ends. That failure *becomes* our destination.[1]

If we are not willing to keep trying to get up, then we will never grow in character and ideals. If we are

---

1. Brandon Sanderson, *Oathbringer* (Tor Books, 2017), pp. 1291–1292.

not willing to fall, then we will never be able to achieve true happiness.

An inspiring story in this regard is that of Jean-Marie Vianney, the parish priest of the French village Ars-sur-Formans. Born in 1786 in Dardilly, a small village near Lyon, he came from a poor family. At an early age, he realized that God was calling him to become a priest. First he had to convince his father, because he had another plan for his son, which was to become a shepherd. When he finally received permission, he entered the seminary. There young Jean-Marie faced a greater challenge: He was not much of a student and he had great difficulty with Latin, even though all the subjects were taught in this language and the exams also had to be taken in Latin.

He was expelled from the seminary because he was unable to reach the desired level of academic performance. Thanks to the mediation and efforts of a priest, Fr. Balley, who did not doubt the boy's priestly vocation, Jean-Marie finally finished his studies with much pain and effort (and with much help from this priest), so that he could be ordained a priest after all.

The diocese, not knowing what to do with this inexperienced and dumb priest, just sent him as pastor to the village of Ars-sur-Formans, near Lyon. Ars had no more than 250 inhabitants and most of the villagers were usually not to be found in the church, but mainly at the pub and dance parties.

After much effort, prayer, and sacrifice, the people in the village became more pious. His fame grew. During his lifetime, masses of people from all over France and even abroad came to Ars to this "dumb" priest for the sacrament of confession and for spiritual guidance. He changed many lives. St. Jean-Marie Vianney was canonized by Pope Pius XI in 1925. And Pope Benedict XVI declared him the patron saint of all priests in 2009.

The story of the "Curé of Ars" can help us on our way to the ideals we want to achieve. If Jean-Marie had already given up when his father resisted his decision to go to seminary, he would not have been able to achieve those high ideals. The same would have happened if he had given up when he failed in his priestly studies for the first time. And also if he had become discouraged and not persevered with his pastoral work in the village of Ars.

This book is not written for people who are perfect; for people who know how to persevere without fail; for people who do not stumble on their way to true happiness. It is written for sinners, for the imperfect, for the weak. For people who fall. Here's another example: the rash and overconfident apostle Peter, whom Jesus chose to lead his Church.

Peter was weak and afraid and he even betrayed the Lord. Another apostle also betrayed the Lord: Judas Iscariot. For thirty pieces of silver Judas was willing to help the Pharisees capture Christ. Both Peter and Judas became aware of their betrayal and both were overcome with grief, but there was a very important difference between them. Peter was able to translate his grief into repentance. Judas translated his grief into despair and eventually even suicide.

Peter became the rock upon which the Church was built. Him! The traitor! The fearful weakling! The one who fervently claimed to be willing to go into prison and death with the Lord and who cowardly walked away when it became real. Yes, Peter became the visible face of Christ on earth, for he is one of history's greatest examples of what it means to be a Christian: trial and error. He sank deep into the mire of sin, but he looked up and saw Jesus standing there reaching out his hand to him. He grabbed the strong hand of God that lifted him up, and with the power of grace he continued his struggle.

Over the centuries, an image of saints has developed that, in my opinion, does not reflect reality at all. You read the craziest stories about holy men and women. As if they were weird people, almost angelic figures who performed strange miracles and were immune to sin. That's not true! Saints were people like you and me: They laughed and cried, they enjoyed this world, they had to fight hard against their weaknesses, and they had to get up very often, because they fell very often. See what St. Josemaría Escrivá said about this: "Saints are not abnormal cases to be studied by a modernistic doctor. They were—they are—normal: with flesh like yours. And they conquered."[2]

---

2. Josemaría Escrivá, *The Way* (Scepter, 1992), no. 133.

I could also have told you the story of Mary Magdalene and of Dismas. Of Augustine of Hippo and of Pelagia. Of Margaret of Cortona and of Camillus de Lellis. All normal people who had fallen deeply into sin, but who eventually managed to rise with a contrite heart and become a saint with God's grace and much struggle.

Holiness is open to everyone. No one can claim, "God created me to be mediocre," or "I am not worthy of becoming a saint." Of course you are worthy! You are worth all the blood of Jesus Christ! And God is your Father! A Christian has no right to give up on his way to the great ideals, to Christ. It doesn't matter if you have few or many talents. Whether you are intelligent or dumb. Strong or weak. You can struggle and you have been given the means by our Lord to get up when you fall.

In the Church we have been given some wonderful means by the Holy Spirit to receive his grace abundantly, the sacraments. Two of them bear a close look because they are very important in our daily struggle of falling and getting up. Those are confession and the Eucharist.

Confession is the sacrament through which we wipe the slate clean and begin our struggle again. Repentance and confession of sins help open the heart to God's help through grace. In the priest, Christ gives the confessant all the grace of the Heavenly Father. It is a wonderful thing and it is also necessary for a Christian who wants to become holy.

In addition to this jewel of God's mercy, another treasure which the Church gives us is the Eucharist. This sacrament is the center and root of the Christian life. It is the most radical expression of Love. Think about it: God gives his own flesh and blood to us so that we may receive him; that we may deify ourselves; that we may make of our lives a loving sacrifice. St. Maria Faustina Kowalska beautifully describes this "foolish" love of God:

> On leaving the earth, O Lord, You wanted to stay with us, and so you left us yourself in the Sacrament of the Altar, and you opened wide your mercy to us. There is no misery that could exhaust you; you have called us all to this fountain of love, to this

> spring of God's compassion. Here is the tabernacle of your mercy, here is the remedy for all our ills.[3]

We have no reason to despair, no matter how great the difficulties in our lives, no matter how tough the challenge we face, no matter how great our fall. God our Father, through the sacrament of confession, always reaches out his hand to us so that we can get up. He never leaves you alone, for he offers himself to you in the Holy Sacrifice of the Mass, that you may become one with him.

---

3. Maria Faustina Kowalska, *Diary of Saint Maria Faustina Kowalska: Divine Mercy in My Soul* (Marian Press, 2019), no. 1747.

4
CHAPTER

Freedom to Love

> It is not so much that we are too bold to endure rules; it is rather that we are too timid to endure responsibilities.
>
> —G. K. Chesterton[1]

The Bengali writer Rabindranath Tagore wrote the following story in his poetry collection *Gitanjali*. A poor man was begging by the roadside. Suddenly he saw the king's golden cart approaching in the distance. His heart was filled with hope. He was looking forward to a great handout that would lift him out of his miserable condition. The cart stopped in front

1. G. K. Chesterton, *What's Wrong with the World* (Dover Publications, 2007), p. 154.

of him. The king looked at him and smiled. The beggar felt how happiness had come into his life. But then the king reached out and asked the poor man, "Can you give me something?" The poor man was stunned. "How can Your Highness think of such a thing! You are begging from a beggar!" The poor man was confused. He had a bag of cereal grains and took a grain out of the bag and gave it to the king. The king got back into the cart and rode on. That evening the beggar emptied his sack. To his great surprise, he saw a golden grain among all the dirty grains. And he cried hot tears. For he realized that the king had returned to him in gold what the beggar had given him. He realized that he had not had the heart to give the king all the grains![2]

There is something confrontational about love. I have said before that it does not consist merely of a good feeling, a nice experience, or a moment of pleasure. Love is painful, vulnerable, uncertain. This is because love is not inward, but outward. It is an act

2. R. Tagore, "Gitanjali" in *Complete Works* (General Press, 2017).

of abandonment. You open the most important vault inside yourself, and take out the most precious treasure, and give it to someone else. The risk is that the other may discard, damage, or reject the treasure. The beggar in this story did not realize until too late that the king would give him back much more than he would take away. The beggar was confused and uncertain. He chose the sure thing. In retrospect, he realized that his cowardice had deprived him of something much greater, and he wept bitter tears.

Love is a paradox. It is a precious treasure that grows larger to the extent that you give it away. And vice versa, it gets smaller to the extent that you keep it for yourself. Let's use an example. In the first chapter, I wrote about great ideals. Unconditional love between husband and wife is one of the greatest ideals there is. Imagine this. A boy and girl like each other. They begin to date and get to know each other better, and they notice that something special begins to emerge. They fall in love. Gradually they share more with each other: time, attention, dialogue, and also intimacy. They make themselves more vulnerable and they increasingly dare to open their hearts to each other with personal feelings, thoughts, and memories that they do not readily share with others. The words, the looks, and the mutual contact are unique.

Such a love can go several ways. Because, at the beginning, every moment together and every thought of each other is full of beautiful feelings, making the relationship go naturally, so to speak, without too much effort. But as the relationship progresses, then you get used to each other and expectations start to arise: commitment, loyalty, duties. Also the willingness to make sacrifices for each other and to put up with each other, even if you don't feel like it. You can then choose to put limits on love anyway. You can choose not to give your whole heart to each other, but instead only part of it. You can choose to make the surrender temporary. But you can also decide to make love unconditional at some point, especially in marriage. In doing so, you choose not to impose conditions on the other person when you give your heart to him or her. You tell the other person: "It's for you, no matter what." The first choice makes love smaller, because you want to keep your heart for yourself when it was not created for that. The second choice makes love bigger and bigger, because you are willing to give your heart away completely, filling it with the love of the other heart.

This fact is intense. Because when you give your heart completely to someone, you are opening yourself up and making yourself vulnerable. Giving your heart away completely is not a passive or a one-time action. It is not that by saying, "here's my heart," you then love that person unconditionally. No, it is a slow and laborious process that takes a lot of time, sacrifice, and energy.

To follow a great, true, and beautiful ideal requires your whole heart, your whole soul. To want to give your heart completely to a person, you need character. To actually do it, you need freedom. But what exactly does that freedom entail? Because these days you hear everyone talking about the value, yes, even the holiness of freedom. Often freedom is described in terms of possibilities: The more opportunities I have to choose, the freer I am. This approach is not wrong, but it is incomplete. Something very important is missing, namely the purpose of freedom. The Christian definition of freedom is the capacity to do good, to love. This definition implies that there are multiple options, because I can be free to choose the good if there is also another option. But it adds a purpose: You are free because you are called, above all else, to do the good.

If freedom is limited purely to open possibilities and to autonomy ("I can do what I feel like doing"), as is often assumed in today's society, then it becomes a licentious freedom, without weight, without direction, without ideals outside oneself. Such freedom is mediocre and insecure. Mediocre because it does not encourage the person to come out of himself, but only to do what he feels like at that moment. Insecure because he cannot test the possibilities he has against a greater good that is outside himself. He is ultimately on his own. Unfortunately, we see this strongly reflected in our individualistic society. Especially among young people, there is a great crisis of freedom because they have no clear references outside of themselves to make important life choices. They are left to their own devices, without a foothold. This can lead to burnout, depression, anxiety, and so on. Even worse, it can lead to being less likely to give one's life to a great loving ideal, because such an ideal requires unconditional choices. They set autonomy and non-commitment higher than unconditional love. Or perhaps they do not set it higher, but do not believe that unconditional love is really possible. No one has explained to them that it is actually possible.

Real freedom does not depend on something external, on the amount of possibilities you have. Real freedom depends on an inner capacity always to choose the good over the bad. This is why the ancient Greeks saw freedom primarily as self-control. For a person who is able not to give in to the impulses, whims, and conveniences of the first moment, but who knows how to pursue higher goals through self-control, is truly free to do the good.

This means that freedom can become greater or smaller, but not to the extent that a person has more or fewer options. It becomes larger or smaller to the extent that a person acts well or badly. For example, if a person often lies, he will be less able to be sincere. A person who is always selfish with himself is less able to be a good friend to another. And if a person is accustomed to wasting his time, he will have less inner strength to study and work hard.

I want to share with you an inspiring explanation of inner freedom. Etty Hillesum was a Dutch Jewish woman who lived through the horror of Nazism. She died in Auschwitz in 1943. At the beginning of the Nazi occupation of the Netherlands, when more and more restrictions were imposed on Jews, she wrote the following in her diary:

> This morning I cycled along the Station Quay enjoying the broad sweep of the sky at the edge of the city and breathing in the fresh, unrationed air. And everywhere signs barring Jews from the paths and the open country. But above the one narrow path still left to us stretches the sky, intact. They can't do anything to us, they really can't. They can harass us, they can rob us of our material goods, of our freedom of movement, but we ourselves forfeit our greatest assets by our misguided compliance.

> By our feelings of being persecuted, humiliated, and oppressed. By our own hatred. By our swagger, which hides our fear. We may of course be sad and depressed by what has been done to us; that is only human and understandable. However: our greatest injury is one we inflict upon ourselves. I find life beautiful, and I feel free. The sky within me is as wide as the one stretching above my head. I believe in God and I believe in man, and I say so without embarrassment.[3]

Christ has revealed to us that we are called to his Love. He has wanted us to be free so that we are not forced to love him, because love is reciprocal. Freedom, then, is God's gift to man to respond to his Love. In doing so, God wants to run the risk of being rejected. Or worse, that man uses freedom purely for himself or to do harm to others. I think that the morality proclaimed by the Church is also much better understood from this perspective of freedom. Freedom has as its

---

3. Etty Hillesum, *An Interrupted Life: The Diaries, 1941–1943; and Letters from Westerbork,* (Picador, 1996), pp. 144–145.

goal, love. Morality helps us make the right choices on our way to that love. Morality is not tormenting. On the contrary, it is liberating!

To give your heart completely to a loving ideal, to love a person with all your heart, you need freedom. To use that freedom well, you need knowledge of morality and, of course, virtues (which I spoke about a few chapters earlier). But you also need something else, and that is trust.

Trust is essential in our relationship with Christ. Our faith is neither a feeling nor an idea. Christian faith is a relationship with a Person. And that relationship will grow stronger to the extent that there is more trust. If you do not regularly interact with Christ through prayer and the sacraments, and if you do not make the effort to delve into Christian doctrine, how will you be able to say a full and unconditional "yes" to him?

A person who takes the time to pray day in and day out (no matter how dry his heart is, no matter how busy he is); a person who makes the effort to regularly receive Christ in the sacrament of the Eucharist;

a person who seeks God's mercy as soon as possible in the sacrament of confession when he falls and wants to get up again; a person who takes the time to immerse himself in the person and message of Christ, that person is one who will persevere in his ideal. For that person has the freedom to give all his heart to God.

5
CHAPTER

Taste Pure Love

The 1960s are known for the so-called sexual revolution. Western youth rebelled against traditional society and introduced social change with the ideal of "sexual liberation." Inspired by thinkers such as Wilhelm Reich and Alfred Kinsey, they would free man from a narrow-minded morality that had prevailed for centuries. It was a bomb that exploded in the West and would have many consequences, including for the Church. Priests, theologians, and laymen began to wonder whether Christian morality about sexuality had become obsolete and whether the Church should not adapt to these new times.

The teaching authority of the Church tried to make clear to the Catholic faithful and to all the world that

Christian sexual morality is not oppressive, but instead is liberating and that it is the way to true love. Thus, Pope Paul VI wrote the encyclical *Humanae Vitae* in 1968 to positively and clearly set forth the Church's teaching on sex and marriage. Several decades later, Pope John Paul II held a series of catecheses on the theological significance of the human body, but even today, many people, including Christians, find it difficult to understand and to live.

Why does the Church cling to this so-called "antiquated" teaching on sexuality? Why won't the Church adjust her doctrine to present-day standards? Why doesn't the Church free the faithful from the difficulties of a chaste life? One can answer these questions from different angles, but the most important one, in my opinion, is that the Church is fully convinced—even in this day and age—that her vision of the human person and his body is fully consistent with the teachings of Christ himself. This teaching of Christ fulfills the deepest desires of the human heart, because they are desires that correspond to the ideal of love to which he has called every person. I will elaborate on this vision so that it can help you better shape your ideals of love and pursue them with greater vigor.

Man is a relational being. By this I mean that human beings are made for relationships; this lies at the core of being a person. Man was not made for solitude. In the book of Genesis, Yahweh says, "It is not good that the man should be alone; I will make him a helper fit for him" (Gn 2:18). And why is man relational? Because he is created in the image and likeness of God. God is not a supreme Being who lives in solitude in the heavens and occasionally engages with his creatures. The Christian God is essentially relational because he is Love.

Two thousand years ago, the Second Person of the Holy Trinity became human. Christ came to earth to free man from sin and to build a bridge between God and man. God became a man of flesh and blood so that through that same flesh and blood we can participate in the eternal love of the Holy Trinity. From this, we can draw an important and profound conclusion: The physical and carnal parts of man are intrinsically good, indeed holy! For Christ himself assumed a body of flesh and blood.

In the sacrament of the Eucharist—which is the foundation of life in the Church—we are invited by Christ himself to receive and eat his flesh:

> He who eats my flesh and drinks my blood abides in me, and I in him. As the living Father sent me, and I live because of the Father, so he who eats me will live because of me. (Jn 6:56–57)

This also clearly shows that the Church does not disdain the carnal. If Christ—who is perfectly human—gives his Body to man in the sacrament of the Eucharist, how could our human body be anything bad?

The most important and fundamental identity of man is that he is made for love. As I have explained in the previous chapters, love is above all self-giving. This means that man is destined to give himself to another. That self-giving leads to union. Union with the Triune God and with other human beings.

It is in this context that we can properly understand the Church's teaching on sexuality. Sexuality is an expression of love between two persons. Love longs for unconditionality, wanting no limits to self-giving.

For it wants to lead to more and more union. Our sexuality is a powerful stream of pure water. To the extent that we know how to channel it, we will enjoy it more and it will bear more fruit.

If we want that stream of water to flow powerfully and well, we must build a firm and impermeable path beneath it and also clear barriers, so that the water does not randomly flow in all directions, but keeps flowing in the right direction. That path where the water can flow is the sacrament of marriage. Marriage is an unconditional covenant that man and woman enter into with God's grace to form a living community together. This community is inherently directed toward the welfare of the spouses and toward producing and raising children.

So is the Church saying that there is no love present in people who have sex outside of marriage? No, the Church is not saying that. It may be that those persons love each other very much and that the relationship they have with each other is also meant to be an expression of love. But that sexual intercourse lacks the unconditionality of love. It lacks a fundamental covenant, a permanent yes. If those two people were to separate and then have relations with others again, that flow of water would lose more and more power and purity, because that power comes from the capacity for self-giving. Self-giving is more powerful when it is unconditional.

In addition, sexuality also has another fundamental dimension and that is procreation. That sex can lead to new life is not an issue. The question is, how does the dimension of procreation relate to that of loving union? The Church says those two dimensions should always go together. The unconditional loving union leads precisely to the spouses not wanting to place limits on the new life that God may bestow. Regardless of intentions and reasons for use, contraceptives are a limiting factor of the love union. The water will flow with less power and it will also become murkier, as you put dikes or obstacles in the route to the true destination.

In the previous chapter, I wrote that knowledge of morality is liberating because it enables us to love. This, of course, also applies specifically to sexual morality.

It is not true that people who live according to the Church's morality have less freedom or are oppressed. On the contrary, they are freer. For they have in that morality a wonderful instrument for tasting pure love. They are thereby able to see God in their own persons and in all other persons to whom they relate.

Nowadays, it is a great challenge to live chastity well. It is not enough that you master this virtue personally and that you put in the necessary means to avoid falling into sin. You must also swim against a current of social misunderstanding and of pressure and sometimes even of mockery. You have to sail through a storm of pornography that has flooded society. But it is certainly possible! Don't listen to those who say that you are putting far too great a yoke on yourself by living this way, or to those who say that true love is a fairy tale. It is not true! Living purely in God's eyes is possible, and it produces deep inner joy and peace.

The holy Curé of Ars once gave a sermon on chastity in which he mentioned a number of ways to live this virtue well. This sermon is two hundred years old, but still very relevant. First, he recommended being vigilant about our eyes, our thoughts, our words, and our actions. This vigilance is a form of discipline and of order. For example, think about your use of the internet. What are you looking at? Why? And also consider how you look at people on the street, what you fantasize about with your thoughts and the conversations you have with others. You may discover that your heart is being fed by all sorts of feelings, images, and ideas, that go against love and feed capriciousness, superficiality, and disordered lust.

His second piece of advice is to resort to prayer. Man's heart is hungry and cannot remain empty. It needs nourishment. The question is: What do you feed it with? A person who prays regularly will fill his heart with the love of Christ. That person will find it much easier to live purely. The same thing happens when two spouses love each other a lot. They feel much less temptation to fill their hearts with sexual thoughts and feelings for others, because their hearts are filled with love for each other.

Third, the Curé of Ars advises us to receive the sacraments regularly. The Eucharist is the sacrament that fills us with the love of the Holy Trinity through the bodily sacrifice of Jesus Christ. We can identify with that sacrifice of our Lord during the Eucharist. This loving sacrifice is a tremendous power to live a pure life, because we can then worship and receive the holy Body of Christ in our own bodies. And we can also be further encouraged to sanctify our bodies after beholding his all-holy and all-pure Body. Therefore, I challenge you to attend Holy Mass not only on Sundays, but also whenever possible on weekdays. Or if you cannot, Eucharistic Adoration is a good alternative.

In addition to the Eucharist, the sacrament of confession is an essential source of love and mercy for a Christian who wants to taste pure love. This applies not only when we fall into sin, but also when we need extra strength in our struggle to live chaste and clean lives. Through confession, we are given the opportunity to begin the battle for pure love with a clean slate. Seize that opportunity as often as necessary!

His fourth suggestion is to flee from everything sinful. If you are restless at night before bed and decide to surf aimlessly on your smartphone, chances are that temptations to watch pornography, for example, will come. Or if you are in a relationship and alone together, the chances increase that you will not be able to resist temptation. As St. Josemaría advises, "Don't be such a coward as to be 'brave.' Flee."[1] Don't be naive and don't act tough. With love you do not take risks; too much is at stake.

Finally, the pastor of Ars heartily advises us to take refuge in our mother Mary. To her I have devoted a whole chapter. I will come back to that. For now, I want to tell you in advance that our loving mother never abandons us when we need her. She always protects us from temptations when we humbly invoke her, and she always leads us to the great Love that is her Son.

In addition to this concrete advice for living chastity well, it is very important to have some other aspects of chastity clearly listed. The first is that the alternative to a chaste life—sexual licentiousness—is

---

1. Josemaría Escrivá, *The Way* (Scepter, 1992), no. 132.

not a beautiful and happy alternative, no matter how strongly some try to make you believe that. The social and cultural influences of recent decades (think of movies, TV series, or pop music, for example) have created the impression that someone who sleeps with many beautiful men or women leads a very happy and successful life. Or that watching pornography is common and even healthy, especially when you are young. This is nonsense! Not only because the Church says so, but also because it is increasingly clear from scientific research that sexual depravity harms your health. For example, pornography has been proven to be harmful to the brain and its addictive effects are similar to those of drugs.[2]

We would do well as Christians to break this sexual taboo. I urge all young Christians to completely shake off any inferiority complex they may have when it comes to chastity, sex, and marriage. A chaste life, driven by love, is an immense source of happiness, joy,

2. Valerie Voon et al., "Neural Correlates of Sexual Cue Reactivity in Individuals with and Without Compulsive Sexual Behaviours," *PLOS ONE* 9, no. 7 (2014), https://doi.org/10.1371/journal.pone.0102419.

and peace. If, on the other hand, a person is guided only by whatever feels good and brings pleasure, and if that person cannot control themselves sexually, he or she will not find deep peace. For his or her behavior goes against the deepest and most loving desires for which man was created.

Another important aspect of chastity is that we should not lose inner peace when we feel temptations. Temptations in themselves are not bad. Sometimes we just feel temptations coming up without consciously seeking them. Don't worry, no matter how strong those temptations are, God allows them. He gives you the opportunity to prove your love for him by joyfully struggling against those temptations. As you overcome them, you will become stronger and, as a result, it will become easier for you to live chastely.

It is true that sometimes we ourselves seek temptation, such as when we watch series or movies that may contain sexually-explicit scenes. Or when we let our imaginations run wild and conjure up sexual images. In those cases, the temptations are the result of foolishness. In those cases, too, we should not lose inner peace. When we haven't been prudent, we can still show God with our efforts that we love him. It's never too late.

And when you sin? As I emphasized in an earlier chapter, the Christian faith is not for perfect people, but for sinners who are willing to get up after every fall and continue to struggle. Go humbly and repentantly to the sacrament of confession and God will shower you with his mercy. Next time, you will struggle with renewed vigor for a loving and pure life. Christ, through your humble and repentant struggle, will always give you a bigger heart, making you stronger in the face of temptations. Worry no more about the past. Every encounter with the mercy of God is a new opportunity to get started.

A characterful Christian is a person who desires to live a chaste life. For chastity produces a pure heart. And people with pure hearts are able to contemplate God's countenance in all people, starting with themselves.

6
CHAPTER

Desire to Listen

> The silence of everyday life is an indispensable condition for living with others. Without the capacity for silence, man is incapable of hearing, loving, and understanding the people around him. Charity is born of silence. It proceeds from a silent heart that is able to hear, to listen, and to welcome.
>
> —Robert Cardinal Sarah[1]

The German author Michael Ende wrote the story of Momo and the Grey Gentlemen in 1973. It is a special story, written for children, but actually intended for adults. Momo is an orphan girl who lives

1. Robert Cardinal Sarah, *The Power of Silence: Against the Dictatorship of Noise* (Ignatius, 2017), no. 20.

in an amphitheater outside an unknown city. She is much loved by the townspeople. They gladly come to see her, because Momo possesses a special talent: She can listen extraordinarily well. By listening attentively, she knows how to give good advice to the people who come to her with their problems.

At one point, gentlemen in gray appear in town who manage to convince people to save their time by working more efficiently and stop doing useless things. They keep the people's time in a bank (actually they steal the time) and as a result they gain power over them. As a result, the economy grows and everyone is more successful. At the same time, everyone lives in a continuous rush and with an unsatisfactory sense, because they have no time to enjoy life and no longer pay attention to each other. The story develops so that at one point Momo is the only one who has not yet sold her time to these gray gentlemen. She will have to save the people from these "time thieves."

The message of the story is clear. It is a critique by the German writer of the modern consumer society, where everyone is always so busy and in such a hurry to do "productive" things (like working, spending, investing, and saving money) that eventually one has little time left to think about why they are doing these things in the first place. These concerns come with a danger: One is easily distracted from important things in life, such as authentic and loving relationships with others.

This critical message from Ende has only become more relevant over time. Technological advances have made us even busier with all sorts of things coming at us. Just think of your smartphone and the amount of notifications, messages, lights, and vibrations you see, hear, and feel throughout the day. If you are not careful, you are busy all day answering messages; bombarded by all the news; looking for information you need and updating others on what is going on in your life. You can spend hours each day wandering around and receiving stimuli in a society that is increasingly fast, rushed, and impulsive.

One of the biggest and most important challenges of today's digital world is to stay calm in the midst of all the rush; to stay focused in the midst of all the distractions; to stay ourselves in the midst of all the social expectations. And that's not easy. Because much of digital technology is designed in such a way that it manages to absorb as much of the user's time and attention as possible. New technologies are designed to be good at distracting us.[2]

Human beings have some precious tools they need to live a meaningful life: silence, attention, and inner calmness. Why are these tools important for becoming happy? They provide depth. If we want our ideals to take proper and firm root in our hearts, they must be allowed to grow deeply. Otherwise, they will topple or blow away at the first setback, negative emotion, or bad mood.

You can see this in friendship. Two friends who can listen well to each other in quiet togetherness, who share much with each other, and who know how to lean on each other, will be much stronger in their friendship when difficulties and setbacks

---

2. This fact has been confirmed by numerous scientists, experts, and former employees of the companies designing this digital technology. Tristan Harris at the Center for Humane Technology is one of the best known. See Center for Humane Technology, https://www.humanetech.com/.

come. For example, when they are separated for a long period of time or when they have a quarrel with each other. In contrast, if two friends base their friendship only on things that bring immediate pleasure, if they pay little attention to each other, and if they are unwilling to patiently take time for the other, their friendship will easily weaken or even crumble at the first setback.

However, you cannot use these tools just like that. They require effort and patience. For example, you cannot taste silence if you do not seclude yourself. To be attentive, you have to know how to protect yourself from distractions. To stay calm, you must first organize and process all the busyness in your head.

I emphasize these ideas of patience, attention, and depth because they are not only enormously important for our human ideals, but even more important for our personal relationship with God, whose foundation is prayer. Especially in this hurried society, I have unfortunately met many times people who have neglected or abandoned their relationship with God because prayer did not produce immediate fruit. Or because prayer felt good at the beginning, but after a while it didn't. Or because they simply did not have the discipline to seclude themselves in silent prayer, without phones, music, or others around them. In some people, it may be a problem of faulty willpower. In others, a problem of trust and patience. In any case, I think many people are unsure how to personally interact with God through prayer. In a way, they have not yet learned to listen.

One who did learn to listen to God was the prophet Elijah. He was fleeing the wrath of Queen Jezebel because he had overcome and humiliated all the prophets of Baal. Earlier, all the other prophets of Yahweh had been killed. He was on his own. After forty days of walking through the desert, he arrives at Mount Horeb exhausted. He goes inside a cave and waits for Yahweh's call to go out and speak to him. The Book of Kings tells what happens:

> And he said, "Go forth, and stand upon the mount before the Lord." And behold, the Lord passed by, and a great and strong wind rent the mountains, and broke in pieces the rocks before the Lord, but

> the Lord was not in the wind; and after the wind an earthquake, but the Lord was not in the earthquake: and after the earthquake a fire, but the Lord was not in the fire; and after the fire a still small voice. And when Eli'jah heard it, he wrapped his face in his mantle and went out and stood at the entrance of the cave. (1 Kings 19:11–13)

Elijah heard God's voice not in the storm, in the earthquake, or in the fire, but in a gentle breeze. The gentle breeze symbolizes silence. In other words, Elijah heard God's voice not in the noise, but in the silence. This biblical story carries a very important message: If we want to hear God's voice we need silence in our hearts.

The foundation of Christian faith is neither an idea nor a holy book. The foundation is a relationship with a Person, Jesus Christ. You and I will be better Christians to the extent that we have a more loving, deeper, and more intimate relationship with Jesus. We all know that in order to have such a relationship, you have to interact regularly with that Person: that you speak to him and, especially, that you listen to him. But God speaks in silence. He whispers. He requires patience and trust.

He is not an impulsive and overwhelming God, but One who, like a gentle and quiet breeze, seeks to speak to your heart in the silence of prayer.

We must be careful, however, not to think of prayer as a Christian form of yoga, as Jacques Philippe warns in his book *Time for God*. Prayer is not a technique that we can use ourselves whenever we want, because prayer is part of love, and love is not a technique for turning inward, like yoga, but a patient and loving search that takes us out of ourselves. It is an encounter with Christ. It is, as St. Teresa of Ávila wrote in her autobiography, "nothing else than an intimate sharing between friends; it means taking time frequently to be alone with him who we know loves us."[3]

Prayer is a gift that God gives to those who have a patient and receptive heart and who humbly ask for it. It is therefore important that we make time for prayer every day, even if we feel dry, even if we don't feel like it, even if we are busy. Even if we have to walk through

---

3. Teresa of Ávila, *The Book of Her Life*, trans. Kieran Kavanaugh, O.C.D. and Otilio Rodriguez, O.C.D. (Hackett, 2008), p. 44.

the desert for forty days, like the prophet Elijah had to do. Even if we are only able to utter simple supplications in prayer such as: "Lord, teach me to pray," "Jesus, in you I trust," or "Come, Holy Spirit." If we pray with such faithfulness and determination, then our relationship with God will no longer depend on our state of mind, on our feelings, or on our whims. Then friendship with Jesus can take a much deeper root in your heart and mine. Someone who lives in close friendship with Christ is someone who has joy and peace.

So how can I pray? How can I shape that trusting dialogue with God without falling into inner monologues or yogic practices? I said earlier that prayer is not a human technique, for prayer is a gift, a gift from God. But there are ways to draw near to God and open our hearts to his Love. Thank God, in the Catholic tradition, we can draw on a tremendous wealth of different forms and types of prayer. Let me highlight two of them.

Meditative prayer is primarily a search for the will of God in your daily life. By contemplating various aspects of your life and asking the Holy Spirit for light, we seek to discover what God desires of us and then try to answer that call. The topic of meditation can be, for example, the Gospel of the day, a liturgical prayer, a text by a Church Father or other Christian writers, but you can also be inspired by a beautiful icon, by nature, or by certain events in your life that have touched you, such as a good conversation with a friend, the advice you received in the sacrament of confession, or a painful event that happened to you recently.

You quietly consider the words, the memories, or the images, and then you ask the Holy Spirit: *What do you want me to do with this? What are you trying to tell me? How can I put this into practice?* This form of prayer has been practiced for centuries (think, for example, of *lectio divina* in the ancient monastic tradition, a meditation based on the Gospel). Since the sixteenth century it has been the basis for many forms of prayer we know in the West.

The second form of prayer is contemplative prayer, the prayer of the heart, of desire, of intimacy. All we want is to be with God, to look at him and experience his loving presence. We do this by seeking silence in our souls, focusing the heart's attention on Christ and contemplating the Love he has for us.

One time we are in Bethlehem, looking with Mary and Joseph at the humble, innocent, and loving face of the Child in the manger. Another time we are a leper receiving a loving embrace from the Lord who heals us of our sickness. Yet another time we kneel with Mary and John before the Cross, where the suffering Christ hangs and looks at us with infinite mercy. Throughout this prayer we try to focus our attention on his eyes, his smile, his hands, his voice . . . on all his being!

What I personally find very beautiful about this form of prayer is that it is also very intertwined with human love. How beautiful it is that two lovers can be endlessly with each other and look at each other without saying a word. With that silent presence, they say more than a thousand words.

Meditative and contemplative prayer are encounters we can have daily with the Lord that will greatly enrich our everyday lives and ideals. In addition, I want to tell you about another practice that is as old as

Christianity itself and that has done numerous people much good: the spiritual retreat. It is a wonderful habit and an effective instrument of God's grace to spend several days of silence in a monastery or in a place of reflection with some regularity (say, once a year).

You may think that the spiritual retreat is something for monks and people who are very pious and mystical. But the fact is that just you and I, normal people in the middle of society, would do well to participate in a spiritual retreat from time to time. After all, you are like a boat sailing through the seas of the world toward your ideals. The boat need only deviate slightly from its route through the distractions of the world to eventually arrive at a completely different destination. A few days of retreat provide you with the map and compass to see if you are still sailing on the right route and what you can do to keep sailing in the right direction. The earlier you detect a deviation, the smaller the change in course needs to be.

Of course, the boat does not always have to stop to get certain insights. Sometimes while sailing you can already see that you need to fix something on the boat or adjust the route a little bit. But some insights you don't get while you are sailing in busy daily life. Sometimes the Holy Spirit wants you to isolate yourself a little longer so that you can properly process all the busyness and noise in your head and in your heart, and so that he can then enlighten you with insights about the choices you make and want to make; about the person you are and are destined to become.

7
CHAPTER

Love the Cross

Whenever you see a poor, wooden cross, alone, uncared-for, worthless . . . and without a corpus, don't forget that that cross is "your" cross—the everday hidden cross, unattractive and unconsoling—the cross that is waiting for the corpus it lacks: and that corpus must be you.

—St. Josemaría Escrivá[1]

One of the most confronting things on earth is human suffering: an illness that happens to us, the death of a loved one, the pain caused by a broken heart, a failed choice of study or career, the loneliness when we have no one around us, and so on. It is not

1. Josemaría Escrivá, *The Way*, no. 178.

easy to deal with suffering itself. Sometimes the fear of suffering is an even greater torment.

Suffering is a mystery. Every human being faces it, but we cannot fully encompass it with our minds. It is beyond our understanding. So is it still worth pursuing big loving ideals, when you know that you could get hit hard and that it may all end differently and worse than you expected? Isn't it better not to have great expectations of this life and not to take too many risks? From the bottom of my heart I tell you: It is worth pursuing big ideals! It's worth embracing all the crosses you encounter in your path. It is worth putting everything into loving self-giving.

But how do we do that? Where do we get the courage to face suffering? The answer to this question is: trust. As I pointed out in an earlier chapter, you can develop trust by getting to know the person you want to trust and by getting acquainted with them. Scottish author Archibald Cronin wrote the book *The Citadel*. It is the story of a young doctor and his wife facing the difficulties of life. At one point in the story, the wife says to her husband:

> But since we're together—oh, since we're ourselves again everything has seemed so clear. It's only when you've got to fight for things that they really become worthwhile. When they just drop into your lap there's no satisfaction in them. Don't you remember those days at Aberalaw—they've been living, simply living in my mind all day—when we had to go through all those rough times together? Well! Now I feel that the same thing is starting for us all over again. It's our kind of life, darling. It's *us*! And oh! I'm so happy about it.[2]

This woman's attitude is fascinating and inspiring. It is not even that she is willing to endure future suffering, she is consciously choosing a life of suffering and she is happy because of it. This idea will come back later.

Sometimes suffering is caused by our own mistakes. For example, an argument you have with someone you love very much or an exam you failed because

2. A. J. Cronin, *The Citadel* (Little, Brown & Company, 1965), p. 337.

you didn't study enough. But it also happens that suffering comes from outside, beyond your control.

You can have several negative attitudes toward suffering: discouragement, cynicism, or indifference. Suffering can lead a person completely astray and can even ultimately destroy their happiness. Yet there are some people who not only manage to "survive" the setbacks in their lives, but for whom suffering has even been decisive in becoming happy, as in the story of *The Citadel*.

Many have experienced at one time or another that adversity has brought us beautiful things in the long run. It is precisely in the difficult moments of our lives that we can appreciate the important things of life even more: love, friendship, family and, above all, God. Someone who lives a life of ease without difficulties is someone for whom it is harder to truly experience what all these things mean. Why is that? Why is it that some people have suffered a lot and yet are very happy while others have an easy life and are not very happy?

According to Christian theology, we have been in God's mind since eternity and he created us to make us happy in his Love. But because of original sin, evil has entered the world. Human nature is damaged by sin. Hence, we do not always do the good we want to do, but the evil we do not want to do, as St. Paul wrote (see Rom 7:15). God has called us to eternal Love. To attain that love, it is necessary for us to purify our hearts from all its evil.

The more our hearts are purified, the more we can love. The instrument to purify man is the cross, it is suffering. Hence, a person who receives many blows in his life, but who knows how to bear these blows with love, is one who is much better able to understand the important things in life.

If we know how to unite our suffering with the suffering of Christ, then our hearts will know how to see better and better. Then we will be able to understand even better how important are things like loyal friends, a united family, or a just society. We will be able to hear more and more clearly what the Holy Spirit whispers in our souls. We will long more and more for the Sacred Heart of Jesus, as we recognize more and more that we were created for his Love.

Loving the Cross of Christ is not a passive act. It is not just waiting for suffering to be sent our way. We can also actively unite ourselves to the Cross of Christ through mortification and penance.

When we make small mortifications out of love for God, we mold our hearts more and more to the heart of Jesus. Our hearts will thereby experience more and more how much God loves us sinners. When we mortify ourselves, we pray not only with our words, feelings, and thoughts, but also with our bodies and senses. We can give that bodily prayer to God as a loving gift. We are then like St. Veronica, who went to Christ with a cloth as he carried the cross toward Calvary. She went to him to lovingly clean his face of all the blood, sweat, and tears with which it was covered. We can also comfort and support the Lord with our mortifications, who in turn carries all the sufferings of man on his shoulders.

What mortifications can you make? I'll list a few examples here so you can get a more concrete picture: At meals, eat less of what you like and more of what you don't like as much. Wait to drink to offer up that thirst. Eat the least tasty piece of fruit from the basket so that others can eat the better fruit pieces. Drink one less beer when you go out with your friends. Smile when you go to school or work in the morning. Get up immediately when your alarm clock rings. Study on time. Take a cold shower. Don't immediately read an incoming message on your phone, but wait a while to offer up that curiosity. Delete a certain application you really like from your smartphone for a certain amount of time. Look in a mirror only when you really need to. Listen to that classmate when he tells an uninteresting story. Don't complain when your mother asks you to do something. And so on.

The wonderful thing is that not only does the practice of small mortifications bear much spiritual fruit, but it is also a wonderful school in the practice of cardinal virtues, especially temperance and strength. You gain much more self-control and discipline in your life. A person who knows how to control himself and who is disciplined has much more freedom and can therefore love more.

8
CHAPTER

Stand Up in the World

> Men of character are the conscience of the society to which they belong
>
> —Ralph Waldo Emerson[1]

A very popular genre, both in literature and cinema, is dystopia. There are all kinds of stories that describe in a critical and pessimistic way what the society of the future will look like. Famous dystopias include *1984* by George Orwell, *Lord of the Flies* by William Golding, and *Fahrenheit 451* by Ray Bradbury. The introduction to this book began with another famous dystopian story, *Brave New World,* by Aldous Huxley.

1. Ralph Waldo Emerson, "Character," in *Ralph Waldo Emerson: Selected Works and Essays,* last modified March 29, 2023, https://emersoncentral.com/texts/essays-second-series/character.

Dystopian stories are often very powerful because they look at society through the lens of a bad idea taken to extremes that the author wants to warn against. Think of a world where personal freedom no longer exists, where major wars destroy society, or where robots gain power over people. In my opinion, dystopias help us to think critically about certain aspects of humans, society, politics, and culture. At the same time, they can also lead to a pessimistic and cynical attitude, simplifying reality into only bad things.

Man's life on earth is a complicated challenge. You do not decide where you are born: It is given to you. All around you, you see that some people are born into difficult circumstances, while others are born into abundance with nothing to complain about. A lot of bad things happen in the world: war, persecution, discrimination, loneliness, poverty, and so on. Therefore, it is not always easy to have an optimistic and loving attitude toward the world you live in.

In addition to the challenges we all share as human beings, Christians also face challenges of their own. Christianity has been prominent in Western European society for centuries. Christianity has shaped the West in many ways. Most people were Christians, and the Church had an important role in people's lives. Today, however, as a Christian, and certainly specifically as a Catholic, you are a minority. It seems as if secular society is really trying its best to erase every trace of the Christian faith from politics, culture, and public life. If it were up to many, religion would only be something for the sitting room, and especially when it comes to Christianity.

Ask yourself how you deal with this condition. As a Christian, how are you supposed to look at the world? How are you supposed to act in a world where so many bad things are happening and where, as a faithful Christian, you also have to swim against the current? The answer is that we should not just tolerate or respect the world in which we live and in which we suffer. No, in fact, we must still love the world. The inspiration for this conviction is the words of God himself in the book of Genesis. On the third day of creation, God saw that it was good. And after the sixth day, he even said that creation was very good. Moreover, in the New Testament we read that God became man, walked around the earth for more than thirty years, and did wonderful things. He is still doing wonderful things! Christ is not sitting on the couch watching from heaven how the world and man go down. He is counting on you and on me to follow his example and to fill this world with his Love, even today!

It would be very sad if Catholics thought of themselves as a pathetic minority that is gradually dying; if we took a "dystopian" attitude and began to look cynically at the world; if we conveniently retreated into the Church without caring about all the problems of people. Pope Francis also spoke very clearly about this during World Youth Day in Rio de Janeiro in 2013. On the Copacabana beach, he told hundreds of thousands of young people: "But the experience of this encounter [with Christ] must not remain locked up in your life or in the small group of your parish, your movement, or your community."[2] And the day before, he said:

> Please, don't leave it to others to be the protagonists of change. You are the ones who hold the

2. Francis, Homily *Holy Mass on the Occasion of the XXVIII World Youth Day* (July 28, 2013), no. 1. Vatican website: www.vatican.va.

> future! You . . . Through you the future is fulfilled in the world. I ask you also to be protagonists of this transformation.[3]

It is easy to sit back and sigh as the Church gets smaller and smaller and the world's problems get bigger and bigger. It is even easier to leave the Church because, according to many people, it no longer belongs to these times. You and I want to be Christians who are willing to work hard to pursue their ideals. Christians who truly have the hope and faith that the world will once again become a place where God's Love is present. Do not be afraid if you think you do not have the talents and tools to fulfill this mission. Do not be afraid because it is not true. You have the talents and you have the resources! In fact, you can work hard and with love, and dedicate that work to the Holy Spirit as a sacrifice so that he can do miracles with it. A saint who spent his life proclaiming this message was Josemaría Escrivá (1902–1975), the founder of Opus Dei.

---

3. Francis, Address *Prayer Vigil with the Young People* (July 27, 2013), no. 3. Vatican website: www.vatican.va.

His mission was to explain how all men and women are called to holiness through the ordinary tasks of life and how in these tasks they can explain to others how to come closer to God. Great was his joy when the Church's Second Vatican Council (1962–1965) proclaimed that all people on earth are called to holiness in the midst of the world, not only the clergy and religious. When he died in 1975, Opus Dei was active on all continents. He was beatified by John Paul II in 1992 and canonized in 2002.

See what this saint said to you and me in a homily on the campus of a Spanish university:

> I assure you, my children, that when a Christian carries out with love the most insignificant everyday action, that action overflows with the transcendence of God. . . . Heaven and earth seem to merge, my children, on the horizon. But where they really meet is in your hearts, when you sanctify your everyday lives.[4]

---

4. Josemaría Escrivá, *Passionately Loving the World* (Scepter, 2004), p. 7.

You and I are Christians who want to change the world around us with God's love. Like the legendary King Midas, who was given the power to turn everything he touched into gold. Thus, we can turn even the smallest things we do into a holy sacrifice for God.

Sometimes the thought may occur to a believer that he is only really a good Christian if he does many things with his parish, with a movement, or with other institutions of the Church. I think it is very good and important for all Christians to be active within Church organizations and initiatives. But we must not forget that our normal activities of every day as Christians in the midst of the world are our main means of becoming holy. This is also our main means of contributing to the Church and making the world a better place. Our daily work is a divine calling that we have all received. In an earlier chapter I talked about the danger of the cloud dweller, who floats around in his life of faith, but who does not have his feet on earth. The Lord wants us to have our feet on earth and our head in heaven and to use our hearts to turn all that is earthly into gold, like King Midas, into the gold of Jesus Christ. We do this by working hard and lovingly.

Let's look at everyday examples. Imagine you are a college student. The alarm goes off at 7:30 a.m. because you still want time to pray and study before your class at 10:00 a.m. You can hit snooze and stay in bed a little longer, or make the effort to get up right away and offer up that sacrifice to God for a specific intention.

A few hours later, you walk to college. Waiting at a traffic light, you notice a homeless person. You can ignore him and cross on the green or go to him, say hello, and offer something with a smile. Then continue to class. You can sink into your chair, use your laptop for distraction, and make a minimal effort to follow the lecturer's explanation, or you can start the class with a quick prayer and dedicate it to God, then do your best to follow the class as attentively as possible so that this can be a worthy offering to God.

In the afternoon, you sit in the library studying. You are ready for a break. You see an acquaintance at the coffee machine. You can walk by and sit on a bench to watch videos on your phone or you can walk over to ask her how she is doing. Once you finish studying, you walk home. You feel like putting in your earbuds and listening to some nice music. But you can also use the route home to pray the Rosary.

In the evening, you have arranged with a group of friends to have a bite to eat and watch a movie together at someone's house. You have countless opportunities to show service and love for your friends: you can pick the least comfortable place to sit; you can get up during the movie to get drinks for the rest; after the movie, you can help leave everything neat and clean the kitchen. While doing all that, you can whisper beautiful short prayers to the Lord.

With these examples, I want to show how you and I, normal people in the middle of society, can turn the everyday things that concern us into a beautiful prayer to God. To do this, we don't have to do weird things. We just have to do our daily duties with love for God and others. That is the essence. Someone who struggles determinedly to live for Christ and asks for help from the Holy Spirit will be able to discover his

Love everywhere, especially in the little things that are seemingly unimportant, such as the alarm clock, a conversation at the coffee machine, or where you sit during a movie.

It is highly important for Christians to be very engaged in society: at work, at the tennis club, at the student fraternity, in a political party, and so on. Christians should not isolate themselves from all earthly matters, but be very involved, and with much love. In this way, you and I will let the light of Christ shine in all human activities. For that divine light to shine in the world, it is necessary that we carry that light within us. If we would be Christians of character, we need to make time daily for our personal relationship with Christ. We should take time for prayer daily, we should receive the sacraments regularly, we should do small mortifications. If Christ does not live in us, then neither can we seed the world with his love and his peace.

9
CHAPTER

Love Your Friends Deeply

Recall the chapter about how God relates to everything with love. Man too is a relational being. Man feels the essential need to relate to others; to have light shined on his existence through others; to live and be together. One of the most beautiful expressions of this desire engraved in our hearts is friendship. A friend is someone you love as they are, with their own personality, background, and life mission. At the same time, you also relate that person to your own individual existence. You choose to give that person a place in your life and ideals and vice versa: He or she allows you into his life. You could say that a friend is a person whom you have chosen as a traveling companion for your path on earth. Even though their path is different from yours, you mysteriously manage to walk together. In other words, you unite your heart with that of the friend without losing your authenticity.

It is not surprising that friendship has always had an important place in literature. Some writers have described friendships in their stories that evoke recognition and admiration. Think, for example, of Don Quixote and Sancho Panza, Sherlock Holmes and Watson, Jane Eyre and Helen Burns, David Copperfield and Agnes Wickfield, Frodo, Sam, Merry, and Pippin, Harry Potter, Ron, and Hermione, and so many more fine examples. It is moving and inspiring to see how the characters in these stories manage to find joy and pleasure in life by being with each other; how they are willing to make the necessary sacrifices for the other; how they manage to face adventure, suffering, and the future together.

Friendship is something you get to know mainly through the experience itself. A person with good friends knows better than anyone else what a friend is worth. Still, I think literature can also teach us deep and valuable lessons about friendship. It is also much needed in these times, because the individualism that has taken such a deep root in our society threatens to erode friendship and limit it to a kind of exchange for personal utility and pleasure. Whereas friendship is so much more!

Friendship is a form of love. As I have explained before, love has something paradoxical about it. It is a precious treasure that becomes more filled as you empty it. Of course, it is true that you can develop a friendship without sharing your heart and soul, but even then the principle applies: That which you share also determines the quality of the relationship. Let's take a couple of examples.

Two young people are in the same class and share a passion for certain video games. They become friends because they share typical school adventures and also because they enjoy gaming together. They can also talk a lot with each other about it. The friendship makes their time at school more enjoyable and also makes them enjoy gaming more. But if the friendship is limited to those two things, then it will also provide no more than entertainment, and it becomes fragile. Imagine if they are both done with school and they also stop gaming regularly, then chances are that the friendship will gradually become diluted and that it will lose its meaning.

Another example. In this case, the two young people met at the same tennis club. After training sessions and matches, they often bike home together because they live close to each other. At first, they mainly share their passion for tennis and the typical things of everyday life. But gradually they also share other things: other hobbies, studying together, and good conversations about life. They also visit each other regularly, so they also get to know each other's families well. The bond becomes stronger and no longer dependent on that which had created the friendship: tennis. If one of them decides to stop playing tennis at that club, chances are the friendship will continue to grow and they will help each other and accompany each other in happy and sad moments.

In the first example, the two friends have shared little with each other. At least, few things of essential importance. The contents of the treasures they gave each other shone for a time, but in the end there was little of value among them except good entertainment. In the second example, the treasure they shared with each other grew larger and more precious. The preciousness was not only in all the beautiful experiences and memories, but also in the fact that the treasure came from their hearts and souls, from their intimacy. Their relationship thus became unique. As they continue to nurture their relationship through time with service, vulnerability, good conversations, and regular acquaintance, the friendship will become more and more unique. It will enrich them both more and more, as the other person's soul always sheds new light on their own. Here we encounter another paradox: The more you give of yourself to a friend, the better you will get to know yourself and the more you can grow in character.

Two very important aspects of friendship are recognition and admiration. On the one hand, you recognize things about your friend that you can relate to in your own life, such as their joys and sorrows, challenges and ideals. On the other hand, you discover in your friend things that you admire and that are exemplary to you. The recognition helps you accept yourself as you are. The admiration helps you continue to grow into who you want to be. Good friendship is therefore one of the most wonderful schools of character building. It truly makes you a better person.

How wonderful it is that we can also apply all these ideas to our relationship with Christ! Christ is our friend. He wants to establish a personal unique relationship with each of us. He is not content with a "little" friendship; He wants to share everything: ideals, dreams, desires, joys, sufferings, and sorrows. He wants to share his Family with you: the Holy Trinity, his Mother Mary, and his Church. He even wants to share his own flesh and blood with you in the sacrament of the Eucharist. Moreover, he fervently desires that you also share all of your life with him. He goes so far that he even wants to become dependent on you. He is willing to suffer pain because of your free will, if only this gives him the chance to receive friendship from you.

If you want to be a Christian of character, if you want to walk the path of holiness, friendship with

Christ is also necessary. The English priest, Robert Hugh Benson, wrote the following about it:

> Now the consciousness of this friendship of Jesus Christ is the very secret of the saints. Ordinary men can live ordinary lives, with little or no open defiance of God, from a hundred second-rate motives. We keep the commandments that we may enter into life; we avoid sin that we may escape hell; we fight against worldliness that we may keep the respect of the world. But no man can advance three paces on the road of perfection unless Jesus Christ walks beside him. It is this, then, that gives distinction to the way of the saint.[1]

How beautiful then are the words of Jesus that we can read in the Gospel of John!

> Greater love has no man than this, that a man lay down his life for his friends. You are my friends if you do what I command you. No longer do I call you servants, for the servant does not know what

1. Robert Hugh Benson, *The Friendship of Christ* (Scepter, 2001), p. 20.

> his master is doing; but I have called you friends, for all that I have heard from my Father I have made known to you. (Jn 15:13–15)

Christ became human so that we can identify with him. At the same time, he remained God so that we can admire him. He is a divine bridge, made of flesh and blood that connects our earthly existence with our heavenly calling. He wants to interact with you, get to know you, and share with you the sufferings and joys of life.

In the end saints are sinners who have a very personal and intimate relationship with Christ. That relationship encourages them to get up when they fall; to give more than what is strictly necessary; to want with a burning desire to help others draw closer to Christ. Saints are people who care more about the suffering and joy of Christ and their neighbor than their own suffering and joy. They love God and their neighbor so much that there is no room in their hearts for self-love.

It is important to have good Christian friends, on whom you can lean and with whom you can share the highest ideal of your life, the Love of God. St. Francis de Sales wrote beautiful words about this:

> For those who live in the world and desire to embrace true virtue it is necessary to unite together in holy, sacred friendship. By this means they encourage, assist, and lead one another to perform good deeds.[2]

How logical and natural then that you would want to share the greatest treasure in your life—the love of Jesus Christ—with your good friends, because you are convinced that a life with God is the greatest happiness! Help your friends to open their hearts to the love of God. That is what the Church calls apostolate. With our example, our confidence, and our advice we can help the other person to open their heart to the voice of the Lord. We can show our friends how to listen to God. If your friends see that you are happy and that you possess joy and peace, and if at the same time

---

2. Francis de Sales, *Introduction to the Devout Life,* trans. John K. Ryan (Image Books, 1972), pp. 175–176.

they see that you are also a normal person in whom they can recognize themselves, then hopefully the desire will arise in them to discover the source of that happiness, that joy and that peace. Through this path of friendship and trust, people will gradually come to know Christ as they come to know the source of love in your person.

What apostolate is ultimately about is loving your friends dearly; that your friends really notice that you care deeply for them; that they see that despite all the uncertainties, setbacks, and pain of this earthly existence, you are deeply happy and joyful; that you want to share that happiness and joy with them.

10

CHAPTER

Realize You Need Help

When we are no longer able to change a situation . . . we are challenged to change ourselves.

—Viktor Frankl[1]

I have already explained ideas several times using examples from literature. A good story contains wisdom and life experiences that are not tied to a specific era, culture, or circumstance. They are applicable to every person. In literature, therefore, you frequently come across a pattern in which the protagonist gets help from someone who is like-minded, who knows

1. Viktor Frankl, *Man's Search for Meaning* (Beacon Press, 2006), p. 112.

him or her well, and who has wisdom and life experience that is valuable to the protagonist.

If we look at real life, we see that many people also use a coach, a mentor, or a trainer to develop themselves personally or professionally and to achieve certain goals. Indeed, the greater the responsibility a person has to bear, and the more important the goal they want to achieve, the more likely they will call on someone to guide them. Top athletes have a personal trainer to help them develop to their full potential. Managers regularly call on coaches to help them deal with certain situations. Many students seek a mentor or a teacher who can orient them in study-related matters.

A person who realizes that he needs help to achieve important goals in his life and actually reaches out to get that help is a person of character. Instead of making excuses or putting off important things, he takes responsibility for what he wants to achieve. In doing so, he shows determination, humility, and openness. It is remarkable that relatively few people seek help and guidance when it comes to the most important thing in life: eternal happiness. It is easy to take refuge in a sense of uncertainty or ambiguity regarding faith and the big questions of life. It sounds even contradictory that someone is considered a wise and prudent person if he says that he cannot know whether there is a God and an afterlife, nor that man's life has a supernatural meaning, nor that one can speak of natural laws and objective morality. On the contrary, the wise and the prudent consult with people who are wise, who have experience, and who have clear guidelines on these big questions!

In the Christian tradition, spiritual guidance has always been an essential means of sanctification. The Church believes that the Holy Spirit speaks through concrete people to help you and me discover the will of God in our lives. I once heard a beautiful quotation, "God has his preferences: What he can accomplish through others, he does not do alone." This idea has a biblical foundation. Throughout Scripture, we see how God has used people to make his will known to others and to help them. Think, for example, of the prophet Samuel, who delivered God's messages to King Saul and King David; think of John the Baptist, who prepared his disciples and all the people of Israel for the coming of Christ. Think of Ananias, who healed Paul of his blindness and helped him find his way in the Christian life.

If we look at the lives of the saints, we see that spiritual guidance has always played an essential role in their path to holiness. For example, the Spanish saint Antonio Maria Claret (1807–1870), who as a young man led a busy life focused on earthly ideals, was deeply touched in his soul one day during Holy Mass, but he did not know what to do with it. He sought refuge at the local Philip Neri House and there he encountered Father Amigó, who was able to guide him in his vocation. Once in seminary, he gained many insights thanks to the advice of Bishop Corcuera. He would eventually become a bishop and founded the Congregation of Missionary Sons of the Immaculate Heart of the Blessed Virgin Mary (the Claretians), an organization that is active in more than sixty countries.

Or look at St. John Bosco (1815–1888). When in doubt about which path to take in his life, he made the decision to become a priest thanks to the advice of a priest friend. Already fully engaged in his pastoral work with young people in Turin, he relied heavily on the spiritual guidance of Father Pelato. Don Bosco would eventually found the Congregation of Salesians, which already had about a thousand vocations at his death.

St. Faustina Kowalska (1905–1938), the Polish nun and mystic who had regular visions of Jesus and Mary and contributed so much to the devotion to Divine Mercy, went very regularly to her confessor, Blessed Michał Sopoćko, for spiritual guidance. Actually, she wrote the following in her diary:

> And now when I hear people sometimes say that they have no confessor; that is to say, a director, fear takes hold of me, because I know very well how much harm I myself experienced when I did not have this help. It is so easy to go astray when one has no guide![2]

2. Maria Faustina Kowalska, *Diary*, no. 61.

The need for spiritual guidance arises when we become aware of several things. First, that our own self-knowledge is not sufficient to walk the path of life toward God's love. We often tend to judge ourselves too harshly or too mildly. Or we overestimate or underestimate aspects of our lives because we don't know how to put everything in its proper perspective.

Second, that we will gain more self-knowledge and wisdom when we allow ourselves to be helped by another. In other words, when we really open up to another. Man is a relational being. He is not made for solitude. So this also means that man becomes more human, so to speak, to the extent that he relates to others. He will discover more about himself when he is in relationship with others, for that is inherent to his nature. The perspective of another can shed new light on our existence that we would never discover in solitude.

How do you find a good spiritual director? Look for someone who has good and thorough knowledge of the faith, who has sufficient life experience, who himself leads a stable and exemplary life of faith, and who humbly trusts the Holy Spirit. This is because it is important that you can truly lean on and trust the counsel you receive. It can be the priest of your parish, a monk or a nun of a congregation you know, someone who is very dedicated to a good apostolate, or a good and pious friend.

How do you know if spiritual guidance is bearing fruit? How do you know you have found the right person?

> The confirmation that we have made the right choice is: when he benevolently helps us find God in all the events of our lives, and makes our will one with God's will, even if we have to make sacrifices for it.[3]

If you have found such a person willing to accompany you on the path to holiness, then you have found a great treasure that you should not lose. Because it really can make a big difference in your life to have such a person beside you, as has been the case with the aforementioned saints.

---

3. Francisco Fernández Carvajal, "La persona adecuada" in *La dirección espiritual* (Palabra, 2012). Our translation.

At the same time, fruitful spiritual guidance does not come automatically. There are several conditions to make it so. First of all, that you take it seriously and do not see it merely as a non-committal opinion for when it is convenient. Regularity in conversations is very important, because regularity keeps the inner struggle alive. In addition, it is very important that you always be very sincere and tell the very things that you would rather keep to yourself and that you may be ashamed of. Spiritual guidance bears fruit in a humble and simple soul that does not want to keep anything hidden from the person who is the instrument of the Holy Spirit.

Another condition is to listen and act on the advice and suggestions you hear. Obedience today is often considered a lack of freedom and character. Of course, obedience can be accompanied by a lack of character and freedom, but then it is also no longer a virtue. Intelligent obedience is the virtue by which we freely detach ourselves from our contrary opinions and are willing to adopt the opinions of a concrete person, believing that this brings us closer to our ideals. Therefore you can say that to practice obedience as a virtue requires a lot of freedom and character. It takes a lot from a person to obey someone else out of intrinsic motivation, without being obliged to do so, out of the humble conviction that he cannot do it alone.

When Christ was praying in agony in the Garden of Olives, realizing that he must face inhuman agony, he pleaded with his Father: “If it be possible, let this cup pass from me; nevertheless, not as I will, but as thou wilt” (Mt 26:39). Christ is also an impressive example for us in this virtue. He even went to the extreme: “He humbled himself and became obedient unto death, even death on a cross” (Phil 2:8).

Obedience in spiritual guidance should not be passive, but proactive. When a person longs to be a good follower of Christ, he will also long for the spiritual director to shed as much light as possible on everything going on in his life. Therefore, it is good to share all insights, issues, and doubts about your life with the spiritual director, no matter how small or unimportant they may sometimes seem. For it is often precisely the small things that help the spiritual director arrive at correct insights.

So don't be afraid to share what you think are finicky things. Leave the judgment of importance in the hands of the spiritual director. He or she will communicate to you whether something was really a small thing and why. This is how St. Faustina Kowalska writes in her diary:

> There is nothing light in the spiritual life. Sometimes a seemingly insignificant thing will disclose a matter of great consequence and will be for the confessor a beam of light which helps him to get to know the soul. Many spiritual undertones are concealed in such things.[4]

What can help a lot for fruitful spiritual guidance is to prepare the conversations in advance in the presence of God. For example, you quietly go over what has happened in your life since the last time you spoke to the spiritual director, and you write down the most important things. You can also examine yourself using a list of topics or a questionnaire related to your faith life. This is because if the conversation in spiritual

4. Maria Faustina Kowalska, *Diary*, no. 112.

direction depends on what spontaneously comes to mind at that moment, you run the risk of the conversation only being about things that evoke emotions at that moment or are fresh in your mind, when those things are not necessarily the most important ones to discuss. Moreover, this prevents you from just having a convivial chat, because spiritual guidance is not meant to be a form of catching up with a friend.

A logical conclusion that follows from this is that a person who regularly reflects on what is happening in his life and how he deals with it is a person who becomes much more self-aware and self-knowledgeable. A concrete way to build that self-awareness and self-knowledge is to take a few minutes every night before going to sleep to go through the day and evaluate: What happened today? What did I do well? What did I do poorly? And what could I have done better? Did I get closer to my ideals? If you do that day in and day out, then you will also be able to open your heart much more consciously and effectively to the spiritual director. Then the Holy Spirit will find much more room in your heart to let his light shine.

A Christian is consciously aware that by personal effort alone he cannot achieve an ideal beyond the natural. He knows that he needs help and he seeks that help, convinced that God will speak to him that way and help him.

11
CHAPTER

Experience Motherly Love

> Only after the Last Judgment can Mary rest a little. Until then, she is far too busy with her children.
>
> —St. Jean-Marie Baptiste Vianney[1]

One of the most fascinating events of the twentieth century took place in a small Portuguese village, Fatima. The Blessed Virgin Mary appeared there six times between May and October 1917 to three simple shepherds, Lucia, Francisco, and Jacinta. Lucia was ten years old, Francisco nine, and Jacinta seven. The last

1. Quote attributed to St. Jean-Marie Baptiste Vianney.

time she appeared to the little shepherds about seventy thousand witnesses were present. At the request of the children, Mary allowed a spectacular miracle to happen. The journalist Avelino de Almeida reported on the event in the Portuguese newspaper *O Século*:

> To the amazed eyes of those people, who, pale with astonishment and with heads uncovered, face the blue sky, the sun trembled, the sun had never-before-seen brusque movements beyond all cosmic laws—the sun "danced," according to the typical expression of the peasants.[2]

This miracle was impressive. But the messages the children received from Mary that they had to convey to the local bishop were even more so. Mary warned that many people go to hell because they refuse the merciful Love of God and will not repent. The children were to pray a lot and make sacrifices for the conversion of all sinners.

---

2. Avelino de Almeida, "How the Midday Sun Danced at Fatima," in *World Apostolate of Fatima: England and Wales,* last modified February 2018, https://worldfatima-englandwales.org.uk/the-miracle-of-the-sun-at-fatima.

She announced the end of World War I, and also warned of a bloody revolution in Russia that would do much harm throughout the world and also the beginning of an even greater war. A few months after the apparition, the communist revolution began in Russia and a few decades later World War II began.

In history, Mary has appeared often to concrete persons to convey a message. I am thinking of her apparition to Bernadette de Soubirous in Lourdes, to Juan Diego in the Mexican village of Tlatilolco, and to Catherine Labouré in Paris. What all these messages have in common is that they come from a loving mother. A mother who fervently longs for all her children to be saved and to enjoy eternal happiness with her son Jesus Christ forever. She warns, she intercedes, she protects. Mary is a gift of God's Mercy. She is the most effective intercessor in history.

Life can be complicated. In theory, we can have a clear picture of where we stand, of how we want to go through life, of the ideals we want to achieve. But in practice, we often run into unexpected things. We have to deal with our own limitations, weaknesses, and falls, as well as events that come upon us and confront us with suffering, uncertainty, and woes.

Christ realizes this and says to us: "Behold thy mother" (Jn 19:27). With this, he tells us, "I give my mother to you so that you can always reach me and receive my love. Indeed, sometimes you are completely lost and don't know what to do. In those cases, you can always grasp Mary's motherly hand and she will always bring you to me, because all of her being is united with me." Mary is daughter of God the Father, mother of God the Son, and bride of God the Holy Spirit. At the same time, she is our mother. A mother who connects our earthly path and our heavenly destiny.

The saints realized this very well. It is touching to see how lovingly and simply they dealt with her. Without shame. With so much trust. Because, as I wrote in an earlier chapter, the saints are also sinners like you and me. And like you and me, they also need a mother. A mother who never leaves them, no matter how sinful they are. Mary makes no distinction between persons. She loves everyone with all her heart.

A person who deals confidently and lovingly with Mary will also deal more and more intimately with Jesus Christ. You can never have too much devotion to Mary, because she always brings your prayers to her Son. Dealing with her is a very enriching way of dealing with Jesus Christ. As St. Josemaría Escrivá wrote: "To Jesus we always go, and to him we always return, through Mary."[3]

How can we get more acquainted with our mother Mary? In the Church we have some wonderful devotions. One of them I want to explain in a little more detail: the Holy Rosary. The Rosary is a vocal prayer in which you consider the Gospel of Christ by contemplating with Mary the most important events in his life. For each event (or mystery), an Our Father, ten Hail Marys, and a Glory Be to the Father are prayed.

Traditionally, the 150 psalms of the Bible were prayed in the monasteries—in some daily, in others spread over several days. The people wished to pray along, but did not know the psalms. The Hail Mary

---

3. Josemaría Escrivá, *The Way*, no. 495.

became popular beginning in the twelfth century, and soon the tradition of praying 150 Hail Marys developed, as a kind of breviary for the people. With other words, the Rosary emerged as a true popular devotion.

I cannot describe the importance of the Rosary for the Christian faithful better than how Lucia of Fatima, the eldest of the three shepherds, did:

> Praying the Rosary is for everyone, rich and poor, learned and ignorant, great and small. All people of good will, can and should pray their Rosary daily. Why? To put us in touch with God, to thank him for his benefits and to ask him for the graces we need. Given that it is necessary for all of us to pray, God asks us, as a daily measure, to pray a prayer that is within our reach: the Rosary, which one can pray as much together as separately, as much in church before the Blessed Sacrament as at home or alone, as much on the road while traveling as on a quiet walk in nature.
>
> Furthermore, I believe that after the liturgical prayer of the Holy Sacrifice of the Mass, the

> Rosary, because of its origin and the exaltedness of the prayers of which it is composed and the mysteries of salvation that we remember and contemplate at each mystery, is the most pleasing prayer that we can offer to God and the most beneficial for our souls. If this were not so, Our Lady would not have recommended it again and again.[4]

Besides the Rosary, there are many other beautiful prayers, devotions, and feasts focused on the mother of God. The Church celebrates a number of beautiful feasts in her honor, such as her Divine Motherhood on January 1, her Assumption on August 15 and her Immaculate Conception on December 8. In addition, there are beautiful prayers that have been prayed for centuries. Consider the *Angelus* prayed daily at noon and the *Memorare* prayed for all those in need.

Another widely spread devotion in the Catholic Church is wearing the scapular of Our Lady of Mount Carmel. In the mid-thirteenth century, Mary appeared

---

4. Gerard van den Aardweg, *Honderd jaar Fatima* [*One Hundred Years of Fatima*], chap. 1 (Stichting De Boog, 2017). Our translation.

to the superior general of the Carmelite order, British saint Simon Stock. She told him that anyone who would wear the scapular of the order until death would be saved from hell. A scapular is a shoulder garment worn over the habit within some monastic orders. Many believers who felt connected to the Carmelite order also wished to wear the scapular. In this way, wearing the scapular of Our Lady of Mount Carmel gradually grew into a popular devotion. For people who did not belong to the order, the scapular was reduced to two square patches connected by shoulder ribbons. Later, it was also adopted in the form of a medal worn on a chain.

There are many other ways to deal with Mary. I find it moving to see how every region and culture in the world has made devotion to Mary so much its own. There are so many beautiful paintings and images of Mary that represent her so differently depending on where they come from. For each has their own representation of Mary. Seeing a procession in honor of Our Lady in Spain, Mexico, or the Philippines makes you aware of this in a very visual way. Mary makes sure that all Catholics around the world remain united with each other and at the same time she enriches everyone in their own individuality, as only a good mother could do.

This book contains many exhortations and challenges. It is meant to confront you a little and give you a nudge in the right direction. As Christians, we have much to do. When you feel lost, turn to Mary with simple and loving words, as a little child would to its mother. Seek comfort and encouragement from her. You will find that gradually you will regain the motivation to continue your struggle to be a characterful Christian who wants to become holy in the middle of the world.

Appendix

Get Started Now

The purpose of this book is to make you aware of the wonderful challenges a Christian faces in today's society. Hopefully, it has led to self-reflection and renewed motivation. The Church and the world need determined Christians who are an authentic light in the midst of society.

I don't know where you stand on your path and in your ideals. Perhaps you are already walking steadfastly and joyfully on the road that is meant for you. Perhaps you have a clear vision of the path you want to walk, but you are not yet sure how to begin. Perhaps you have no idea yet which path is meant for you. It could also be that you have been walking on a road that leads to a wrong destination for some time and you are looking for a turn to a right road.

In any case, it is a sign of character that you are not putting off possible resolutions, but are trying to take concrete steps in the right direction today. Keep moving. Don't stand still. Otherwise, laziness and mediocrity will creep into your soul and eventually motivation and good intentions will fade away.

Here are some suggestions to get started.

1. *Regularly seek help in the sacraments and in spiritual guidance.*

   On your own you cannot succeed. Without God's grace in the sacraments (especially in confession and the Eucharist) and without spiritual guidance, it is difficult to begin, to continue, and to persevere.

2. *Make room in your daily life for defined times of prayer.*

   A Christian needs prayer. Prayer needs quietness, time and space in your heart. Do not let your prayer depend on spontaneity, on good feelings, on convenience. It will happen to you more often than not that you are busy, have other priorities, or don't feel like it. Make it a regular, recurring appointment with the Lord. For example, pray for ten minutes every day at the beginning of the morning.

3. *Make a good schedule for each day so that you spend your time well.*

   Laziness and boredom are great enemies of character. They lead to mediocrity. Try to spend your time well each day. Plan time for relaxation too. You will find that you have more energy and motivation for your ideals.

4. *End your day with an examination of conscience.*

   I recommend ending the day with a few minutes of silent reflection in the presence of God: How was my day? Did I put my resolutions into practice? What can I do better tomorrow? End with an act of contrition, asking the Lord for grace to start again joyfully the next day. The examination of conscience keeps you sharp and your inner struggle alive.

5. *Read good books about the faith.*

   As Catholics, we have an incredible wealth of wisdom and knowledge in our tradition! It is worth spending time regularly on spiritual reading.

If you are still not sure where to start, I recommend the following books:

- The Bible: It is important that as a Christian you learn the Bible well, especially the New Testament. Regularly meditate on the gospel stories, because Christ speaks to you through his life and his word.
- The *Catechism of the Catholic Church*: A thick work that looks dry and boring, but in my opinion is the finest and most complete summary of the Catholic faith. Don't try to read it to the end, but take your time to let each paragraph sink in.
- St. Francis de Sales, *Introduction to the Devout Life*: It was written from the conviction that a devout life is for everyone and is not reserved for those with a special vocation or state of life.

- St. Josemaría Escrivá, *The Way*: Short, challenging, and concrete reflections on all kinds of topics related to the Christian life that encourage the reader to meditative prayer and self-reflection.